green drinks

green drinks

Sip your way to five a day with more than 50 recipes for great-tasting smoothies and juices

with recipes by
Nicola Graimes

RYLAND PETERS & SMALL
LONDON • NEW YORK

Designer Maria Lee-Warren
Editor Kate Eddison
Production Controller Sarah
Kulasek-Boyd
Art Director Leslie Harrington
Editorial Director Julia Charles
Publisher Cindy Richards

Indexer Hilary Bird

First published in 2015
by Ryland Peters & Small
20–21 Jockey's Fields
London WC1R 4BW
and
Ryland Peters & Small, Inc.
519 Broadway, 5th Floor
New York, NY 10012
www.rylandpeters.com

10 9 8 7 6 5 4 3 2 1

Text © Nicola Graimes, Pablo Uribe,
Louise Pickford, Anya Ladra,
Dunja Gulin, Jenna Zoe, Amy Ruth
Finegold, Tonia George, Maxine Clark
and Ryland, Peters & Small 2015.
Design and photographs
© Ryland Peters & Small 2015

ISBN: 978 1 84975 604 4

Printed and bound in China

A CIP record for this book is available
from the British Library.

US Library of Congress cataloging-in-
publication data has been applied for.

Neither the author nor the publisher
can be held responsible for any
claim arising out of the information
in this book. Always consult your
health advisor or doctor if you have
any concerns about your health
or nutrition.

Notes
• The recipes have been created
with adults in mind; if serving them
to children, omit the superfoods and
dilute half and half with pure or
filtered water.
• All spoon measurements are level,
unless otherwise specified.

Contents

juicing basics

By enjoying fresh, raw green juices, smoothies and blends on a regular basis, you are on the path to good health, and with the addition of superfoods, you are on the superhighway to rejuvenating and invigorating both mind and body. Whether you're looking for a potent pick-me-up, an effective detoxifier or an anti-ageing rejuvenator, this book shows how to make flavour-packed juices, smoothies and blends with these – and many other – therapeutic properties.

What makes green drinks different from other smoothies and juices?

Along with the nutrients gleaned from fresh fruit and vegetables, these great-tasting drinks contain the added benefit of active superfoods, or super-nutrients, such as spirulina, wheatgrass and chia seeds. Green drinks are also naturally lower in sugar than other fresh fruit juices and smoothies, using nutrient-rich green vegetables such as spinach, kale, cabbage, broccoli, watercress, cucumber, avocado, lettuce, peas, rocket/arugula, basil, parsley and celery. With the addition of sweetness from apples, pears, melons, grapes and other vitamin-packed fruits, these drinks are as tasty as they are healthy.

The benefits of making your own green drinks

There is no comparison between home-produced juices and store-bought drinks from a health point of view; with homemade drinks you know what you're getting, you can choose your favourite fresh produce, they are additive-free with no added sugar and they're not pasteurized, which can deplete their nutritional status. Homemade juices can be described as liquid fuel, nourishing the body with a potent combination of vitamins, minerals, antioxidants, phytochemicals and enzymes. As well as giving a nutritional boost, juices, smoothies and blends have the ability to cleanse the liver and kidneys, revitalize flagging energy levels, flush the body of toxins, boost immunity, de-stress, rejuvenate the mind and body and aid weight loss.

Tips for juicing success

To ensure that you get the most from your juicer or blender, let's go back to basics by explaining the difference between a juice, smoothie and blend. The former is made by passing fresh raw vegetables or fruits through a juicer, which extracts the fibre to provide a readily digestible, nutrient-laden juice. Smoothies, on the other hand, are made by pulverizing fresh raw produce into a pulp in a blender with yogurt, milk or a dairy-free alternative, while a blended drink replaces the dairy element with juice, water and the like; either way, the end result is thicker than a juice and also retains valuable fibre/fiber, although the nutrients take longer for the body to absorb.

• Choose fresh produce that is in season and at the peak of ripeness, as the juice, smoothie or blend will not only taste superior but will also be at its nutritional best. Conversely, avoid under-ripe, old, wrinkly or damaged fruit and vegetables. Buy fresh produce from a retailer with a steady turnover, to ensure you know that it hasn't been sitting on the shelf very long. Better still, grow or pick-your-own fruits and vegetables!

• One of the goals of drinking juices is to flush out toxins from the body, so it makes sense to avoid using foods that contain unwanted additives, chemicals, pesticides and fertilizers, and use organic fresh produce instead. If the purse allows, the health benefits and often the taste are well worth the extra cost. If using non-organic fresh produce, wash it well. Also choose unwaxed citrus fruit or alternatively scrub it thoroughly before use.

• It's not always necessary to remove the skin from fresh produce before blending, and as most of the nutrients lie in or just below the skin, it pays to leave it on whenever possible (obviously if the skin is very thick or inedible, this isn't an option). The skin will make the blend slightly fibrous, but I don't usually find this an issue when you take into account the health benefits.

• Some juicers may struggle with leafy vegetables and herbs, so an easy solution is to roll them into a bundle or wrap them around a more juicy vegetable or fruit before putting them through the machine. For maximum juice extraction if you have a centrifugal juicer, soft or particularly juicy fruit and vegetables, such as berries, peaches, pears, melon or cucumber, can be put through the appliance twice.

• Homemade juices, smoothies and blends do not tend to keep well and should be drunk soon after making, as their flavour, texture and nutritional value diminish with exposure to light and oxygen. You can add lemon juice to extend their life slightly, if you like, but they are still best consumed shortly after making.

• Fresh juices can be strong-tasting and potent, so if you have a delicate digestive system or are not used to drinking them, dilute with pure or filtered water before drinking. The recipes have been created with adults in mind; if serving them to children, omit the superfoods and dilute half and half with pure or filtered water.

• Superfoods can be bought in various forms, from fresh to tablets, capsules and powders. For convenience and consistency, the recipes in this book use green superfoods, such as spirulina, chlorella and wheatgrass, in powdered form. The dosage given in each recipe is perhaps conservative, but if you have not taken superfoods before, it is advisable to start off with small quantities and then increase the dosage after a period of time when your body becomes more attuned to them. That way, you can monitor any reaction you have to consuming them. It is also recommended to compare the quantity of superfood specified in the recipe with the dosage on the pack, as strengths can vary. Follow the instructions on the pack, if in doubt. For herbal remedies, again check the recommended dosage on the pack. For more information on green superfoods, see pages 10–11.

juicers & blenders

Juicing tools and equipment have come a long way in recent years, but which piece of equipment you choose to buy largely depends on your budget and what you need from your appliance.

Centrifugal juicer

This juicer works by using a flat cutting blade in the bottom of a rapidly spinning basket, which shreds the fresh produce and flings the pulp to the sides of the basket or into a separate container, while the juice passes through the small holes into a jug/jar. If you are making a small amount of juice, there is an advantage to using a centrifugal machine, as it does not eject the pulp but continues to work until the basket is full, so it reduces the amount of cleaning. This type of appliance does vary in its juice yields, but it is quick and convenient. Choose a model with a robust, high-powered motor to handle the high-speed extraction process.

Masticating juicer

This type of juicer effectively shreds or 'chews' vegetables and fruit, releasing their juices. It is extremely effective in extracting juice and tends to be more proficient at handling leafy greens and herbs than a centrifugal model. However, for some people, it is preferable to have a juicer and a separate wheatgrass/leafy greens machine, possibly hand-operated, to cover all bases. Masticating juicers tend to produce juices with a reasonable nutritional shelf-life, as they incorporate less oxygen in the juicing process than centrifugal machines. Opt for a sturdy appliance with a reliable, powerful motor and it should last you for many years. Also choose one that is easy to clean and put back together afterwards. Most machines come with various attachments that allow you to make ice cream, mill grains and grind nuts, for instance, so bear this in mind when considering your options.

Blender

If you intend to use your blender on a regular basis, it pays to invest in a sturdy, heavy-based model with a powerful motor, as it will certainly make light work of smoothies and blended drinks that include firm fruits and vegetables. Other factors you may wish to consider are whether the jug/jar is the right capacity for your needs and that it is sturdy with a tight-fitting lid and a hole in the top for adding ingredients. It should also be easy to clean. You may not need a plethora of speeds, but look for an appliance with a range of functions, 3 or 4 speeds and a pulse button; many blenders also have pre-programmed cycles that make them easy and convenient to use, as well as attachments that can grind nuts and spices or mill grains.

Citrus juicer

Expensive equipment is not essential for making citrus juices. The hand-held reamer, citrus squeezer or the more costly citrus press are perfect for extracting juice from oranges, lemons and limes. Many electrical juicers also come with an attachment that can extract the juice from citrus fruits.

Hand-held blender

A hand-held immersion blender is perfect for handling an individual serving of a smoothie or blend, as well as for pulverizing herbs or greens to stir into juices, if your juicer has difficulty coping with fresh leafy stuff. As with a blender, look for a sturdy appliance offering variable speeds and one that is easy to clean.

spirulina

powdered greens

barleygrass

green superfoods

Spirulina

This impressive, highly nutritious, nourishing blue-green micro algae both regenerates and cleanses the body. This is thanks to its rich chlorophyll content, which helps transport oxygen to every cell in the body. It is one of the highest sources of usable protein and features essential fatty acids, antioxidants, vitamins A, B12, E and K, iron, calcium and phytonutrients in a readily usable and digestible form. Spirulina has been found to treat liver damage, protect the kidneys, enrich the blood, protect the heart, enhance intestinal flora, aid weight loss and inhibit the growth of yeast, fungi and bacteria in the body; an all-round winning combination!

Powdered greens

There are many different brands available and it pays to buy powdered greens from a reputable

retailer and avoid those that include unwanted additives. They shouldn't be seen as a substitute for real leafy greens, but they are a great way of boosting your dietary intake and the nutritional value of juices, smoothies and blends. What's more, many blends contain other potent health ingredients such as chlorella, spirulina, wheatgrass, flaxseeds, alfalfa and probiotics, so you get a super-nutritious conglomeration in one pot. The health benefits vary depending on what you want from your greens mix, so it's possible to buy blends for detoxing, energy-boosting, immunity support or improving digestion, for example.

Barleygrass

With similar therapeutic attributes as wheatgrass (see opposite) and brimming with vitamins and minerals, barleygrass is slightly easier to digest and has a milder flavour than its cereal counterpart. This high-chlorophyll food acts as a free-radical scavenger and also reduces

hemp protein
powder

wheatgrass

chlorella

inflammation in the body. The recipes in this book use powdered barleygrass, but do use fresh, if available and if your juicer can cope with it, as its nutrient content is likely to be superior.

Chlorella

This nutrient-rich green algae helps to detoxify, cleanse, alkalize and protect the body, boosting energy levels as well as vitality. Chlorella encourages cellular renewal, growth and repair, which all decline with age. It features the highest level of chlorophyll of any food, helping to control viral and fungal infections such as candida overgrowth, chronic fatigue and poor immunity. It is also an anti-inflammatory, relieving arthritis pain. Stress, depression, constipation, asthma, poor digestion and high blood pressure have all been found to improve after taking chlorella on a regular basis. Chlorella contains a higher percentage of protein and beneficial fatty acids, including omega-3, than both wheatgrass and spirulina.

Protein powders

Protein plays an essential role in the repair and maintenance of every cell in the body. We're not talking body-building whey powder here but plant-based proteins, such as those made from soya, hemp and pea. Stress, illness, hormonal imbalances and high activity all affect protein requirements, but if your diet contains good amounts of protein, you may feel it unnecessary to supplement.

Wheatgrass

Widely acknowledged as one of nature's superfoods, wheatgrass contains high concentrations of vitamins, minerals, chlorophyll and all essential amino acids, along with digestive enzymes, some of which are not found in other foods. It is a well-known detoxifier, blood purifier and cleanser, but is perhaps less known for its cholesterol-reducing, anti-ageing and anti-inflammatory properties. Wheatgrass is a leafy green, rather than a grain, so it's suitable for those with wheat allergies.

detoxifiers

virgin apple mojito

super green detox

I love the hit from the lime juice and fresh mint in this vibrantly green, zingy juice. This makes a refreshing, cooling drink served on ice, or you could top it up with chilled carbonated mineral water. If serving this to green drink sceptics, they'll never know that the kale is there!

virgin apple mojito

Juice the apples, kale and three-quarters of the mint – add a splash of the lime juice if the juicer struggles with the kale. Stir the lime juice and barleygrass into the juice and pour into 2 glasses filled with crushed ice. Chop the reserved mint leaves and sprinkle over the top before serving.

4 green apples, quartered, cored and cut into wedges
2 large handfuls of curly kale
1 handful of fresh mint leaves
freshly squeezed juice of $\frac{1}{2}$–1 lime
1–2 teaspoons barleygrass powder (see page 10)
crushed ice, to serve

Serves 2

Lemon not only adds a real lift to the flavour of this cleansing juice but it also stops it oxidizing, helping to retain its vibrant colour and nutrients. Wheatgrass, barleygrass or spirulina can all be used instead of the chlorella if preferred.

super green detox

Juice the pears, celery, spinach, kale and cucumber. Stir in the lemon juice and chlorella until combined. Pour into 2 glasses and serve.

2 pears, quartered and cored
1 celery stick/rib
1 handful of spinach
2 large handfuls of curly kale
$\frac{1}{2}$ large cucumber, quartered lengthways
freshly squeezed juice of 1 lemon
1–2 teaspoons chlorella powder (see page 11)

Serves 2

Not for the faint-hearted – you just know that this intensely green juice is doing you good! Choose watercress sold loose in bundles for the best flavour and nutrient value.

green giant

Juice the cucumber, watercress (if your machine struggles with the watercress, add a splash of water or some of the lemon juice) and broccoli florets and stalks. Stir in the lemon juice, olive oil and wheatgrass. Pour into 2–3 glasses and serve.

1 chilled cucumber, quartered lengthways
3 handfuls of watercress
1 head of broccoli, both florets and stalks, chopped
freshly squeezed juice of ½ lemon
½ teaspoon extra virgin olive oil
1–2 teaspoons wheatgrass powder (see page 11)

Serves 2–3

Simplicity in a glass – fresh root ginger gives a real zing to this juice and is just the thing to revive you after a long night! Apple lends a touch of sweetness and helps to balance out the earthiness of the spinach.

apple zinger

Juice the apples, ginger and spinach, then stir in the lemon juice, greens and wheatgrass. Divide between 2 glasses and serve.

4 apples, quartered, cored and cut into wedges
2.5-cm/1-inch piece fresh root ginger, unpeeled
2 large handfuls of spinach
1 teaspoon freshly squeezed lemon juice
1 teaspoon powdered greens (see page 10)
1 teaspoon wheatgrass powder (see page 11)

Serves 2

green giant

green day

Don't waste the stalks from the broccoli, as they are just as good juiced as the florets. Providing a potent combination of super-nutrients, this fruit and vegetable juice is further enhanced by the green algae, chlorella.

spring clean

Juice the broccoli, apples, spinach, celery and spring greens, then stir in the lime juice and chlorella. Divide between 2 glasses and serve.

3 good handfuls of broccoli, both florets and stalks
4 apples, quartered, cored and cut into wedges
4 handfuls of spinach
1 celery stick/rib
4 handfuls of shredded spring greens
freshly squeezed juice of 1 lime
1–2 teaspoons chlorella powder (see page 11)

Serves 2

Brassicas such as broccoli, cabbage and kale contain nutrients that boost the liver enzyme called glutathione, which helps to cleanse the liver of heavy metals.

green day

Put the apple, broccoli, rocket/arugula, cucumber, lemon juice, coconut water and wheatgrass powder in a blender, and blend until smooth. Add a splash of water if too thick. Divide between 2 glasses and serve.

1 green apple, quartered, cored and cut into wedges
4 broccoli florets
1 handful of rocket/arugula leaves
$^1/_2$ cucumber, peeled, deseeded and cut into chunks
freshly squeezed juice of $^1/_2$ lemon
250 ml/1 cup coconut water
1–2 teaspoons wheatgrass powder (see page 11)
a splash of pure or filtered water (optional)

Serves 2

The vitamin C in the lemon helps the absorption of the iron provided by the spinach and parsley. Iron is an important mineral and aids detoxification, which takes place in the liver.

green shot

Juice the spinach, parsley and watercress, interspersing them with the wedges of apple to help them through the juicer, then juice the ginger. Stir in the lemon juice and wheatgrass. Divide between 2 glasses and serve.

4 handfuls of spinach
2 handfuls of fresh parsley
4 handfuls of watercress
3 apples, quartered, cored and cut into wedges
2.5-cm/1-inch piece fresh root ginger, peeled and halved
freshly squeezed juice of 1 lemon
1–2 teaspoons wheatgrass powder (see page 11)

Serves 2

You may be asleep but your body is busy repairing and maintaining itself, so help it on its way with this calming drink. Camomile and lettuce are recognized for their soporific qualities, helping you to sleep well and in turn enhance your body's natural detoxing process.

sleep easy

Make the camomile tea with the boiling water and allow to steep for 5 minutes. Remove the tea bags and allow to cool. Pour the cooled camomile tea into a blender and add the grapes, lettuce and lemon juice. Squeeze the grated ginger through a muslin/cheesecloth bag or your fingers to extract the juice and add the juice to the blender, then blend until smooth. Stir in the milk thistle. Divide between 2 glasses and serve.

2 camomile tea bags
500 ml/2 cups boiling water
4 handfuls of green seedless grapes
2 handfuls of soft leaf lettuce
freshly squeezed juice of 1 large lemon
4-cm/1¹/₂-inch piece fresh root ginger, peeled and finely grated
a few drops of milk thistle (check the recommended dosage on the bottle)

Serves 2

Prunes lend a rich sweetness to this drink, but their real claim to fame is their ability to prevent constipation and improve the intestinal flora of the digestive system. The cleansing prunes are further boosted by the kale, orange juice and spirulina.

feeling flush

Put the prunes, kale, alfalfa, orange juice, lemon juice and spirulina in a blender with the pure or filtered water, then blend until smooth. Add a splash more water if it is too thick. Divide between 2 glasses and serve.

10 ready-to-eat pitted dried prunes, halved
2 handfuls of curly kale, tough stalks discarded, shredded
1 small handful of alfalfa sprouts
300 ml/1^1/$_4$ cups freshly squeezed orange juice
freshly squeezed juice of ^{1}/$_2$ lemon
1–2 teaspoons spirulina powder (see page 10)
100 ml/generous ^{1}/$_3$ cup pure or filtered water

Serves 2

melon, cucumber &
sweet ginger frappé

The melon, cucumber and lime make this a hydrating and detoxifying drink. It has an added kick of spicy ginger to increase circulation. Melon is cooling and hydrating, and is rich in minerals, which carry water into the body's cells.

melon, cucumber & sweet ginger frappé

Scoop the flesh from the melon into a blender. Add the cucumber and the remaining ingredients, and blend until smooth. Pour into a jug/pitcher or 2 glasses and serve.

½ galia melon, about 1 kg/
  2¼ lb., halved and deseeded
½ cucumber, peeled and cut
  into chunks
freshly squeezed juice
  of ½ lime
1 tablespoon chopped
  stem ginger
1 tablespoon ginger syrup from
  the jar
6 ice cubes

Serves 2

We often feel the need to detox after a late night of over-indulgence. Pears are very cleansing and cucumber is the best diuretic around. With the addition of grapefruit, which aids in overcoming alcohol intoxication, you can say goodbye to your hangover with this cleansing drink.

morning cleanser

Press all of the prepared ingredients through a juicer into a jug/pitcher. Stir, divide between 2 glasses and serve.

4 firm ripe pears, about
  650 g/1½ lb, quartered, cored
  and cut into chunks
½ cucumber, cut into chunks
1 small grapefruit, peeled,
  pith discarded, and cut
  into wedges
5-cm/2-inch piece fresh
  root ginger, unpeeled

Serves 2

Unlike most fruit avocado has a high fat content, but it is monounsaturated fat, so will not raise cholesterol levels. Avocados are also rich in lecithin and minerals. The addition of mint adds a refreshing quality to the drink, and this aromatic herb also calms the digestive tract and helps quell nausea – perfect for calming a hangover.

avocado, pear & mint cooler

Scoop out the avocado flesh and put in a blender with the pear juice, mint and lime juice, then blend until smooth. Pour into 2–3 glasses and serve.

1 avocado, halved and
    stoned/pitted
500 ml/2 cups pear juice
leaves from 4 fresh mint sprigs
freshly squeezed juice
    of 1 lime

Serves 2–3

Green tea is a powerful antioxidant. The Chinese and Japanese have used green tea as a medicine for centuries to help treat headaches and poor digestion, improve wellbeing and extend life expectancy. It nourishes the skin and is antiviral and antibacterial. Green tea powder is available from Asian shops and health-food stores.

green tea detox

Put the banana in a blender with the green tea powder and pear juice. Blend until smooth. Add honey to taste, if preferred. Divide between 2 glasses and serve.

1 banana, peeled and cut
    into chunks
2 teaspoons green tea powder
500 ml/2 cups pear juice
1 teaspoon honey, to taste
    (optional)

Serves 2

green tea detox

energy enhancers

popeye special

Spinach contains decent amounts of iron but it is essential to eat a food rich in vitamin C at the same time to help the body absorb the mineral. Thankfully, fresh orange provides heaps of vitamin C, as well as a refreshing zesty tang to this juice.

popeye special

Juice the oranges, spinach and cabbage, and stir in the cooled green tea and basil leaves. Divide between 2 glasses and serve sprinkled with the orange zest.

6 oranges, peeled, pith discarded, and quartered
4 handfuls of spinach
4 handfuls of chopped pointed cabbage
150 ml/²⁄₃ cup green tea, cooled
6 fresh basil leaves, chopped
1 teaspoon finely grated orange zest

Serves 2

The chilli/chile certainly gives a kick to this nutrient-dense juice, which will liven you up for the day ahead. Remove the seeds from the chilli/chile if you prefer a tamer juice!

rocket fuel

Juice the apples, kale, broccoli, carrots, alfalfa sprouts and three-quarters of the chilli/chile. Stir in the lemon juice and powdered greens or barleygrass. Divide between 2 glasses. Finely chop the reserved chilli/chile and sprinkle on top of each glass.

2 apples, quartered, cored and cut into wedges
2 large handfuls of curly kale
1 handful of broccoli, both florets and stalks, chopped
2 carrots, peeled and halved lengthways
2 handfuls of alfalfa sprouts
1 red chilli/chile, quartered lengthways
2 teaspoons freshly squeezed lemon juice
1–2 teaspoons powdered greens or barleygrass powder (see page 10)

Serves 2

Rich, creamy and sustaining, this is almost a meal in itself! Avocados are often misconstrued as being high in fat and therefore unhealthy, but they are brimming with beneficial nutrients and provide lots of energy.

almond & date shake

Put the almond milk, spinach, avocado, dates, tahini and barleygrass in a blender with the pure or filtered water, and blend until smooth. Add more water if too thick. Divide between 2 glasses and serve.

300 ml/1¼ cups almond milk, or milk of choice
3 handfuls of spinach, tough stalks discarded, shredded
1 small avocado, stoned/pitted, peeled and chopped
6 ready-to-eat pitted dried dates, halved
2 teaspoons tahini paste
1–2 teaspoons barleygrass powder (see page 10)
75 ml/⅓ cup pure or filtered water

Serves 2

Peas may be an unusual addition to a smoothie, but the sweet and succulent vegetable is surprisingly good, especially when combined with fresh mint. Frozen petits pois are perfect here, making an incredibly rich and creamy drink, and there is no need to defrost them first.

pea...fect!

Put the petits pois, mint, kale, coconut water, coconut oil and chlorella in a blender, and blend until smooth. Add extra coconut water if it is too thick. Divide between 2 glasses and serve.

3 handfuls of frozen petits pois
2 handfuls of fresh mint leaves
2 handfuls of kale, stalks discarded, leaves shredded
300 ml/1¼ cups coconut water
½ teaspoon virgin coconut oil
½–1 teaspoon chlorella powder (see page 11)

Serves 2

pea...fect!

ginger spice

This lip-smacking juice is best served in shot glasses for an instant kick-start to your day! It will wake you up, clear the sinuses, aid digestion and make you feel energized.

ginger spice

Press all the ingredients through a juicer into a jug/pitcher. Divide between 3 glasses and serve.

½ lemon, peeled, pith discarded, and cut into chunks
1 fennel bulb, about 180 g/ 6 oz., trimmed and cut into chunks
1 apple, quartered, cored and cut into chunks
3-cm/1¼-inch piece fresh root ginger, unpeeled
100 g/²⁄₃ cup green seedless grapes

Serves 3

A green smoothie is the best way to increase your consumption of dark leafy greens. Bananas are added to provide sweetness and lots of energy.

green super smoothie

Place the bananas, kiwi fruit and spinach in a blender, and add the chlorella powder and spirulina powder. Blend until smooth. Pour into 2 glasses and serve.

2–3 ripe bananas, peeled and cut into chunks
1 kiwi fruit, peeled and chopped
2 handfuls of spinach, tough stalks discarded
½ teaspoon chlorella powder (see page 11)
½ teaspoon spirulina powder (see page 10)
400 ml/1²⁄₃ cups pure or filtered water

Serves 2

This green smoothie tastes good enough to be a cocktail, and can transform even the biggest green-juice sceptics. It makes the perfect refresher for a summer afternoon, and will sustain your energy levels through until dinner.

green tropical juice

Put the cucumber, pineapple, parsley and spinach in a blender. Blitz until smooth, then squeeze in the juice of either half or the whole lime, depending on how tart you want your smoothie to taste. Add the stevia and spirulina, and blitz again to mix. Divide between 4–6 glasses and serve.

½ cucumber, peeled and cut into chunks
300 g/scant 2 cups chopped pineapple
a generous handful of fresh flat-leaf parsley
a small handful of spinach, tough stalks discarded
1 lime
1 teaspoon stevia
½ teaspoon spirulina powder (see page 10)

Serves 4–6

This is a great way to get your greens along with hemp, a superfood seed. Hemp is a complete food, containing all the essential amino acids. You can camouflage hemp with a little tropical fruit so that its nutty undertones appeal to all.

sweet spinach & hemp smoothie

Blitz all the ingredients in a blender until you have a smooth, liquid consistency. Pour into a glass and serve.

2 handfuls of baby spinach, stalks discarded
90 g/½ cup chopped pineapple
240 ml/1 cup coconut milk
60 g/½ cup ice
½ frozen banana, peeled and cut into chunks
2 tablespoons milled hemp seeds or 1 tablespoon hemp powder

Serves 1

Starting the day with a glass of this freshly squeezed veggie and fruit elixir will make you feel energized, nourished and light. It contains dark green leafy vegetables, which are packed with vitamins and minerals

alkalizing green juice

Begin juicing all the ingredients, adding a little of the water from time to time (it's always a good idea to dilute pure juice with water to get an isotonic, rehydrating drink). Add the oil to the juice (this will allow all the oil-soluble vitamins to be absorbed), stir and serve immediately in glasses.

5–6 Granny Smith apples, quartered, cored and cut into wedges
380 g/13 oz. or 1 small head of cabbage, sliced
seeds from 2 pomegranates
4 handfuls of green leafy vegetables (dark kale, chard, spinach, carrot greens, parsley, nettles, etc.)
$1/2$ lemon, peeled, pith discarded, and cut into chunks
15 g/$1/2$ oz. fresh root ginger, peeled
about 360 ml/$1 1/2$ cups pure or filtered water
1 teaspoon flaxseed, hemp or other oil

Serves 4–6

wake up & go juice

A potent hydrator and thirst quencher, the cooling cucumber and refreshing mint stimulate the palate and help rid the digestive system of toxins. The naturally rich sugars found in melon and grapes will provide you with a burst of energy.

wake up & go juice

Press all the ingredients through a juicer into a jug/pitcher or large glass and serve.

½ lemon, peeled, pith discarded, and cut into chunks
a small wedge of honeydew melon, about 180 g/6½ oz., peeled, deseeded cut into chunks
½ cucumber, cut into chunks
1 celery stick/rib, cut into chunks
100 g/²/₃ cup green seedless grapes
a handful of fresh mint leaves

Serves 1

When choosing melons, always smell them – a ripe melon's scent is heady and aromatic. Melon is a great diuretic and high in vitamin C. Grapes are also very cleansing – they are alkaline and highly nutritious – and kiwi fruit are packed with essential minerals, especially potassium. This energizing juice tastes sensational.

go green juice

Put the melon and kiwi fruit in a blender. Add the grapes and the leaves picked from the mint sprigs, if using, and blend until really smooth. Serve in glasses over ice.

½ honeydew melon, peeled, deseeded cut into chunks
2 kiwi fruit, peeled and roughly chopped
200 g/1¹/₃ cups green seedless grapes
¼ bunch of fresh mint sprigs (optional)
ice cubes, to serve

Serves 2

pick-me-ups

sweet as...

Nurturing and sustaining, this juice provides a valuable cocktail of nutrients, protein and carbohydrates – just what you need to get you back to good health after a bout of illness. The Peruvian fruit camu camu provides impressive levels of immune-boosting vitamin C.

sweet as...

Juice the sweet potato, Chinese leaves, red (bell) pepper, ginger and pumpkin seeds, adding a splash of pure or filtered water if your machine struggles with the seeds. Stir in the wheatgrass powder or camu camu powder and sprinkle with bee pollen. Pour into 2 glasses and serve.

1 sweet potato, peeled and cut into long wedges
2 large Chinese leaves, each halved and rolled up
1 red (bell) pepper, deseeded and cut into long wedges
2-cm/³/₄-inch piece fresh root ginger, peeled
2 tablespoons pumpkin seeds
1–2 teaspoons wheatgrass powder (see page 11) or camu camu extract powder (available from health-food stores or online)
¹/₄ teaspoon bee pollen

Serves 2

A cross between a smoothie and soup, this makes a nutritious snack or light lunch. It's a delicious, rejuvenating combination of creamy avocado, fresh coriander/cilantro and delicate cucumber with just a hint of fresh chilli/chile.

avocado smoopie

Put all the ingredients into a blender, and blend until smooth and creamy. Divide between 2 glasses and serve.

1 avocado, stoned/pitted, peeled and chopped
¹/₂ cucumber, deseeded and sliced
2 spring onions/scallions, chopped
2 tablespoons chopped fresh coriander/cilantro leaves
1 green chilli/chile, deseeded and sliced
250 ml/1 cup coconut water
a splash of Tabasco sauce
freshly squeezed juice of 1 lime
5 ice cubes
1–2 teaspoons spirulina powder (see page 10)

Serves 2

The green melon varieties used in this drink, galia and honeydew, are both very aromatic and provide a subtle green shade to the drink. The frothy texture contrasts with the ginger syrup – this is a refreshing and hydrating juice.

melon froth

Put the melons through a juicer and transfer to glasses. If using ginger syrup, serve it separately.

1–2 galia or honeydew melons, halved, peeled and deseeded
1 teaspoon wheatgrass powder (see page 11)
ginger syrup, to taste (optional)

Serves 1–2

This bright green nut milk is surprisingly sweet and tasty. Try it – it's a great way to eat your greens and is also pretty filling. It provides an instant energy boost and nourishing pick-me-up.

green nut milk

Put all the ingredients in a blender, and blitz until completely smooth. Divide the nut milk between 2–3 glasses and serve lightly chilled.

400 ml/1^2/$_3$ cups pure or filtered water
150 g/1 cup raw cashews
2 ready-to-eat, pitted dried dates
1 teaspoon coconut oil
^{1}/$_4$ teaspoon salt
1 large handful of spinach, tough stalks discarded

Serves 2–3

This smoothie provides a powerful boost of vitamins, minerals, antioxidants and other nutrients for an instant lift. The melon seeds are high in vitamins A and C, so you can leave them in the smoothie for extra nourishment.

melon, banana, lime & parsley smoothie

Combine all the ingredients in a blender, and blend until completely smooth. Divide between 2–3 tall glasses and serve immediately.

2 bananas, peeled and cut into chunks
200 g/7 oz. galia or honeydew melon, peeled and cut into chunks (seeds attached)
a handful of fresh parsley
freshly squeezed juice of 1 lime
1 teaspoon barleygrass powder (see page 10)
500 ml/2 cups pure or filtered water

Serves 2–3

parsley, orange &
watercress smoothied

mint lemonade

These ingredients are wonderfully good for you and you will love this tangy and fruity flavour with aromatic parsley in the background. Parsley is high in blood-building chlorophyll and iron, beta-carotene, vitamin K, calcium and potassium.

parsley, orange & watercress smoothie

Place all the ingredients in a high-speed blender and purée until smooth. Pour into 2–3 glasses to serve.

200 ml/generous $^3/_4$ cup pure or filtered water
200 ml/generous $^3/_4$ cup freshly squeezed orange juice
120 g/1 cup chopped mango flesh
1 small banana, peeled and cut into chunks
a small handful of fresh parsley
a handful of watercress

Serves 2-3

This uplifting lemonade stimulates the circulation, refreshes the body and enlivens the senses. Serve this on a warm afternoon to tingle your tastebuds and wake you up for the rest of the day.

mint lemonade

Blend all the ingredients in a high-speed blender, strain through a sieve/strainer and chill. Divide between 2 glasses and serve.

freshly squeezed juice of 1 lime
freshly squeezed juice of 1 lemon
400 ml/1$^2/_3$ cups pure or filtered water
1–2 tablespoons raw agave nectar, to taste
a handful of fresh mint leaves

Serves 2

The tingle comes from the ginger, always a refreshing addition to juices. Pears reduce acidity and are one of the least allergenic of all fruits. This utterly delicious combo of apples, pears and ginger is a great way to kick-start your day.

apple, pear & ginger tingler

Press the apples, pears and ginger through the juicer into a jug/pitcher. Serve over ice.

2 apples, quartered, cored and cut into wedges
4 pears, quartered, cored and cut into wedges
5-cm/2-inch piece fresh root ginger, unpeeled
ice cubes, to serve

Serves 2

Fennel can be very difficult to juice – you need a strong machine. Alternatively, chop it and purée in a blender with apple juice, then strain. Use a crisp, sweet, green apple. Always remember to remove the stem and stalk ends of apples and pears, where any pesticides and residues collect.

apple juice with fennel

Trim the green leaves from the fennel bulb, trim off the root end, then slice the bulb into long wedges and cut out and remove the cores from each wedge. Cut the apples into wedges. Put the apples and fennel through a juicer. Stir in the lemon juice to stop discoloration, then serve immediately, topped with a few fennel sprigs for extra scent.

1 fennel bulb, including sprigs of the feathery leaves
2 apples, cored
freshly squeezed juice of ½ lemon

Serves 1–2

apple juice with fennel

weight-loss aids

green for go

Melon and ginger have always been great partners and this refreshing, long drink, topped up with sparkling mineral water, is no exception; it's perfect for sipping, helping to curb the appetite and keep you hydrated.

green for go

Juice the cucumber, melon, kiwi and ginger then stir in the lime juice and sparkling water. Pour into 2 glasses and sprinkle the chia seeds over before serving.

½ cucumber, quartered
lengthways
¼ large honeydew melon,
peeled, deseeded and sliced
2 kiwi fruit, peeled and
quartered
1-cm/³/₈-inch piece fresh root
ginger, unpeeled
freshly squeezed juice of
½ lime juice
100 ml/generous ⅓ cup
sparkling mineral water
¼ teaspoon chia seeds

Serves 2

If you're not a big fan of green leafy vegetables, the rich texture and tropical flavour of the mango and banana are a real boon. This makes a nutritious and sustaining start to the day when you are looking for low-fat breakfasts.

cabbage love

Put all the ingredients into a blender and blend until smooth. Divide between 2 glasses and serve.

2 small handfuls of kale, tough
stalks discarded, shredded
1 mango, stoned/pitted, peeled
and cut into chunks
1 banana, peeled and cut into
chunks
2 tablespoons sunflower seeds
1–2 teaspoons spirulina powder
(see page 10)
400 ml/1²/₃ cups pure or
filtered water

Serves 2

Pineapple is a rich source of bromelain, an enzyme that helps to break down proteins and has anti-inflammatory properties.

pineapple & apple juice with spinach

Starting with a few apple wedges, juice the apples, spinach, mint and pineapple in a juicer. Whisk in the lime juice. Divide the juice between 2 glasses and serve lightly chilled.

**5 apples, quartered, cored and
  cut into wedges
2 handfuls of spinach
1 handful of fresh mint
½ large pineapple, peeled and
  cut into wedges
freshly squeezed juice of
  1 lime**

Serves 2

Here is a refreshing and tangy green juice that combines cooling cucumber with the tart taste of apples and watercress.

cucumber, apple & pear juice with watercress

Starting with a few apple wedges, juice the apples, watercress, cucumber and pears. Whisk in the lemon juice. Divide the juice between 2 glasses and serve lightly chilled.

**3 apples, quartered, cored and
  cut into wedges
2 handfuls of watercress
1 large cucumber, quartered
  lengthways
2 pears, quartered, cored and
  cut into wedges
freshly squeezed juice of
  1 lemon**

Serves 2

pineapple & apple juice
with spinach

minty ginger
granny smith

Any apples will do, but unpeeled Granny Smiths produce the most beautiful green. Just a hint – apple juice adds natural sweetness to drinks, so you will not miss the sugar here. Lime juice will stop the apple juice turning brown so quickly, but drink this concoction immediately – don't let it hang around, or you lose all the benefits of freshly crushed juice.

minty ginger granny smith

Push half the apples through a juicer, then the ginger, mint and lime juice, if using. Finally, push through the remaining apples and serve.

4 Granny Smith apples, quartered, cored and cut into wedges
a chunk of fresh root ginger, peeled and sliced
4–8 fresh mint sprigs
1 tablespoon freshly squeezed lime juice (optional)

Serves 1

Don't let the broccoli in this juice put you off trying it! Apple and the subtle aniseed taste of the fennel are what dominate.

apple, fennel & broccoli juice

Put all the ingredients in a juicer and blitz until all the juice is extracted. Divide the juice between 2 glasses and serve.

650 g/1½ lbs. apples (about 4 large apples), quartered, cored and cut into wedges
200 g/7 oz. broccoli, both florets and stalks, chopped
250 g/9 oz. fennel (about 1 large fennel bulb), trimmed and cut into chunks
1 lemon, peeled, pith discarded, and cut into chunks

Serves 2

When trying to lose weight, sometimes you need something nutritious and filling to really sink your teeth into. Other times you'll fancy something sweet. This is where this smoothie comes in – it ticks all the boxes for a nutritious yet delicious dieter's 'dessert'.

green protein smoothie

Put the milk, yogurt or ice, banana, hazelnuts, spirulina or barleygrass powder and salt in a blender. Blend until smooth. Add a few drops of lemon juice, to taste, and agave nectar, if needed. Pour into 2 glasses and serve.

250 ml/1 cup raw almond milk
125 g/½ cup raw yogurt, chilled, or crushed ice
1 small banana, peeled and chopped
2–4 tablespoons hazelnuts
½ tablespoon spirulina powder or 1 tablespoon barleygrass powder (see page 10)
a pinch of salt
freshly squeezed lemon juice, to taste
½ tablespoon raw agave nectar (optional)

Serves 2

In Chinese medicine, reishi is recommended for regulating and normalizing the function of the main organs of the body. Additionally, it's an adaptogen, so helps to maintain and restore overall balance to the body.

magic mushrooms

Juice the apples, kale, carrots and celery, then stir in the lemon juice and reishi powder. Divide between 2 glasses and serve.

3 apples, quartered, cored and cut into wedges
1 handful of curly kale
2 carrots, peeled and halved lengthways
1 small celery stick/rib
freshly squeezed juice of ½ small lemon
2 teaspoons reishi mushroom powder (available from health-food stores or online)

Serves 2

This super green juice falls into the 'good for you' category popular for January detoxing and weight-loss plans. It is packed full of nutrients from the broccoli and spinach, as well as the superfoods barleygrass and chia seeds, leaving you feeling sustained and energized.

super-duper juice

Juice the apples, spinach, broccoli florets and grapes. Stir in the lime juice, barleygrass and chia seeds. Divide between 2 glasses and serve.

3 apples, quartered, cored and cut into wedges
3 handfuls of spinach
1 handful of broccoli florets
2 handfuls of green seedless grapes
2 teaspoons freshly squeezed lime juice
1–2 teaspoons barleygrass powder (see page 10)
$\frac{1}{4}$ teaspoon chia seeds

Serves 2

cucumber juice
with spinach

Celery juice is marvellous when mixed with other vegetable juices – and also with juicy fruits such as grapes. You can buy grape juice, but fresh juice is a revelation. Green grapes give the drink a lovely green colour and a delicious sweetness.

celery & grapes

Push the celery sticks/ribs into the juicer, leaf end first. Alternate with the grapes, which are very soft and difficult to push through on their own. Press through the watercress, if using, and serve plain, in glasses filled with ice, or put into a blender with ice cubes to produce a delicious celery-grape froth.

6 celery sticks/ribs, trimmed
about 20 green seedless grapes
a bunch of watercress
(optional)
ice cubes

Serves 1–2

Spinach is high in iron, but not in a form easily used by the body, so it needs to be consumed with vitamin C. If you mix it with some delicious cucumber and lemon juice, you'll absorb all its goodness painlessly.

cucmber juice with spinach

Juice half the cucumber, then all the spinach, then the remaining cucumber. Add salt and lemon juice to taste, if using. Pour into 1–2 glasses and serve.

1 cucumber, about 30 cm/
12 inches long, quartered
lengthways
a large handful of spinach
salt and lemon juice, to taste
(optional)

Serves 1–2

skin detox

beauty
boosters

The watercress gives a spicy kick to this vibrant green juice, which is a winning combination created to help tone and beautify the skin as well as give strong, healthy hair and nails.

green goddess

Juice the apples. Using a hand-held blender, blend together the watercress, parsley, alfalfa sprouts and lemon juice, then add to the apple juice and stir in the spirulina. Divide between 2 glasses and serve.

6 green apples, peeled, cored and cut into wedges
4 handfuls of watercress, large stalks discarded
4 handfuls of flat-leaf parsley, stalks discarded
1 small handful of alfafa sprouts
freshly squeezed juice of 1 small lemon
1–2 teaspoons spirulina powder (see page 10)

Serves 2

If your juicer struggles with leafy greens, it's a good idea to alternate adding the greens with the grapes, to help them on their way. Spinach and cabbage are a surprising source of omega-3 fats, which help to keep skin healthy and plump.

skin detox

Juice the grapes, spinach, pears and cabbage. Stir in the lemon juice and powdered greens. Divide between 2 glasses and serve.

2 handfuls of green seedless grapes
4 handfuls of spinach leaves
2 pears, peeled, cored and cut into long wedges
4 handfuls of shredded sweetheart cabbage
2 teaspoons freshly squeezed lemon juice
2 teaspoons powdered greens (see page 10)

Serves 2

This simple green drink is healthy and hydrating, and bursting with 'green power'. Packed with vitamins and minerals to nourish the skin, it also contains extra water to leave you hydrated and full of vitality.

tangy green juice

Put the apple, kiwi fruit, melon, agave nectar, lime juice and cayenne in a blender, and add the water. Process until puréed and smooth. Pour into 4 tall, ice-filled glasses and serve immediately.

1 crisp green apple, peeled, cored and diced
2 kiwi fruit, peeled and sliced
225 g/ 1 cup chopped ripe honeydew melon flesh
60 ml/$^1/_4$ cup raw agave nectar
3 tablespoons freshly squeezed lime juice
$^1/_4$ teaspoon cayenne pepper
360 ml/1$^1/_2$ cups pure or filtered water
ice cubes, to serve

Serves 4

This juice is green, green, green – the green pigment found in these fruits and vegetables, chlorophyll, provides a welcome balance of alkalinity to an over-acidic state. It also helps deodorize bad breath and body odour, counteracts toxins in the body, is anti-inflammatory and improves liver function.

green kiwi juice

Press all the ingredients through a juicer into a jug/pitcher. Divide between 2 glasses and serve.

2 kiwi fruit, peeled and quartered
2 pears, quartered, cored and cut into chunks
115 g/4 oz. wedge of white cabbage, cut into chunks
100 g/3 $^1/_2$ oz. sugar snap peas
100 g/3 $^1/_2$ oz. spinach
a small handful of fresh mint leaves

Serves 2

tangy green juice

lettuce &
parsley crush

Cucumber is hydrating and cooling, while green grapes will give you an energy boost. Basil was traditionally used to reduce bloating.

cucumber, grape & basil juice

Press the cucumber and apples through a juicer into a jug/pitcher. Transfer to a blender, add the grapes and basil and blend until smooth. Pour into 2 glasses and serve.

½ cucumber, cut into chunks
2 green apples, quartered, cored and cut into chunks
250 g/1²/₃ cups green seedless grapes
2 fresh basil sprigs

Serves 2

Lettuce and parsley produce small quantities of juice and taste decidedly green! So add the juice of an apple or other fruit as an extender and sweetener. As many good cooks know, much of the flavour in parsley is found in the stalks, so juice them too.

lettuce & parsley crush

Form the lettuce and parsley leaves into balls and push through the feed tube of the juicer. Push the apple through (this will extract more juice from the lettuce and parsley). Stir if necessary, then serve immediately.

1 cos or iceberg lettuce, stalk trimmed
a large bunch of parsley, including stalks, ends trimmed
1 green apple, quartered and cored

Serves 1

Barleygrass is known to improve the condition of the skin and is helped here by the hydrating effect of the cucumber and coconut water. This makes a refreshing, cooling summery drink, especially if served on ice.

skin freshener

Put the kiwi fruit, cucumber, coconut water, lime juice, mint, quinoa and barleygrass into a blender. Squeeze the ginger through a muslin/cheesecloth bag or your fingers to extract the juice and add to the blender. Blend until smooth.

4 kiwi fruit, peeled and chopped
1 small cucumber, deseeded and chopped
275 ml/generous 1 cup coconut water
freshly squeezed juice of $\frac{1}{2}$ lime
a small handful of fresh mint leaves
2 tablespoons flaked quinoa
1–2 teaspoons barleygrass powder (see page 10)
1.5-cm/$\frac{5}{8}$-inch piece fresh root ginger, peeled and finely grated

Serves 2

Surprisingly tasty; very refreshing; deep, dark green; packed with chlorophyll. If you use more kale and less water, you'll get a very strong, chlorophyll-tasting drink. You can juice celery, parsley or watercress instead of kale. Or use lemons or grapefruit instead of oranges.

dark kale orangeade

Put the kale leaves in a juicer and blend until smooth. Repeat with the oranges. In a big jug/pitcher, combine both juices with the water, oil and agave nectar, if using. Pour into 4 glasses and serve chilled or add ice cubes, if you like.

400–800 g/14–28 oz. dark green kale leaves
4 oranges, peeled, pith discarded, and quartered
1–1.5 litres/4–6 cups pure or filtered water
$\frac{1}{2}$ tablespoon flaxseed oil
2 tablespoons raw agave nectar (optional)
ice cubes (optional)

Serves 4

This is one of the most beneficial of all the juices in this chapter – low in sugar, high in antioxidants and alkalizing, as well as hydrating.

green veggie juice

If you are using a masticating juicer, run all the ingredients through the juicer. If you using a centrifugal juicer, alternate leaves with the celery and apple to prevent them getting caught in the machine. Divide the juice between 2–3 glasses and serve.

1 cucumber, quartered
   lengthways
5 celery stalks/ribs
100 g/3½ oz. broccoli, both
   florets and stalk, chopped
¼ fennel bulb, trimmed
½ courgette/zucchini, trimmed
1 apple, quartered and cored
1 lime, peeled, pith discarded,
   and cut into chunks
3 large handfuls of fresh
   parsley
3 large handfuls of spinach
   or curly kale

Serves 2-3

basil limeade

The flavonoids contained in nutrient-rich basil are thought to have anti-inflamatory effects. The amount of lime and sugar is a personal thing, so you can adjust it to taste, adding more of one or the other as necessary.

basil limeade

Put the lime juice, sugar and basil in a blender (one that is able to crush ice) and blend until smooth. Add the ice and blend briefly to break up the ice cubes. Pour into chilled cocktail glasses and top up with the soda water.

225 ml/1 scant cup freshly squeezed lime juice (from about 10 limes)
75 g/$\frac{1}{3}$ cup packed light brown sugar
a handful of fresh basil leaves
2 handfuls of ice cubes
250 ml/1 cup soda water

Serves 4-6

Kiwis are a secret weapon against colds, being rich in vitamin C. They are sharp and sweet, and mixed with the mellower flavours of pears and apples they make a really gorgeous early-morning juice.

pear, kiwi & apple juice

Pass the pears, kiwi fruit and apple through a juicer, one at a time, into a jug/pitcher. Add enough ice for 2 people and serve.

3 pears, quartered, cored and cut into wedges
3 kiwi fruit, peeled and quartered
1 apple, quartered, cored and cut into wedges
ice, to serve

Serves 2

index

credits

Photography credits:

Jonathan Gregson
Page 60

William Lingwood
Pages 2, 38, 41, 45, 46, 50, 56

Ian Wallace
Pages 6-7, 20, 23, 28, 32

Kate Whitaker
Pages 1, 4, 5, 10-19, 24, 27, 31, 34, 37, 42, 49, 52, 55, 59

Recipe credits:

Nicola Graimes
Virgin Apple Mojito, page 13
Super Detox, page 13
Apple Zinger, page 14
Green Giant, page 14
Spring Clean, page 17
Green Day, page 17
Green Shot, page 18
Sleep Easy, page 18
Feeling Flush, page 19
Popeye Special, page 25
Rocket Fuel, page 25
Almond & Date Shake, page 26
Pea...fect!, page 26
Sweet As..., page 35

Avocado Smoopie, page 35
Green for Go, page 43
Cabbage Love, page 43
Magic Mushrooms, page 48
Super Duper Juice, page 49
Green Goddess, page 53
Skin Detox, page 53
Skin Freshener, page 58

Louise Pickford
Melon, Cucumber & Sweet Ginger Frappé 21
Morning Cleanser, page 21
Avocado, Pear & Mint Cooler, page 22
Green Tea Detox, page 22
Ginger Spice, page 29
Wake Up & Go juice, page 33
Go Green Juice, page 33
Pear, Apple & Ginger Tingler, page 40
Green Kiwi Juice, page 54
Cucumber, Grape & Basil Juice, page 57

Anya Ladra
Green Super Smoothie, page 29
Green Nut Milk, page 36
Melon, Banana, Lime & Parsley Smoothie, page 37
Parsley, Orange & Watercress Smoothie, page 39
Mint Lemonade, page 39
Pineapple & Apple Juice with Spinach, page 44

Cucumber, Apple & Pear Juice with Watercress, page 44
Apple, Fennel & Broccoli Juice, page 47
Green Veggie Juice, page 59

Jenna Zoe
Green Tropical Juice, page 30

Amy Ruth Finegold
Sweet Spinach & Hemp Smoothie, page 30

Dunja Gulin
Alkalizing Green Juice, page 31
Green Protein Smoothie, page 48
Dark Kale Orangeade, page 58

Elsa Petersen-Schepelern
Melon Froth, page 36
Apple Juice with Fennel, page 40
Minty Ginger Granny Smith, page 47
Celery & Grapes, page 51
Cucumber Juice with Spinach, page 51
Lettuce & Parsley Crush, page 57

Pablo Uribe
Tangy Green Juice, page 54

Tonia George
Basil Limeade, page 61
Pear, Kiwi & Apple Juice, page 61